IDAHO

Past and Present

John Stanley

New York

Published in 2011 by The Rosen Publishing Group, Inc.
29 East 21st Street, New York, NY 10010

First Edition

Library of Congress Cataloging-in-Publication Data

Stanley, John.
Idaho: past and present / John Stanley.—1st ed.
    p. cm.—(United States: past and present)
Includes bibliographical references and index.
ISBN 978-1-4358-9480-8 (library binding)—ISBN 978-1-4358-9507-2 (pbk.)
— ISBN 978-1-4358-9541-6 (6-pack)
1. Idaho—Juvenile literature. I. Title.
F746.3.S73 2011
979.6—dc22

2009049391

Manufactured in Malaysia

CPSIA Compliance Information: Batch #S10YA: For further information, contact Rosen Publishing, New York, New York, at 1-800-237-9932.

On the cover: Clockwise from top left: Native Americans from the Shoshone tribe; a farmer plows a field; Idaho's Sawtooth Mountains.

Contents

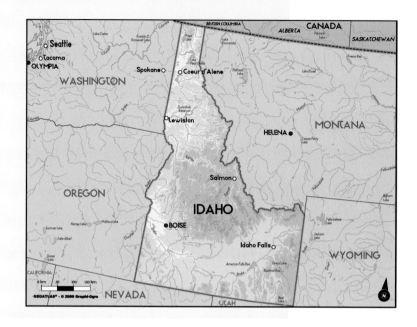

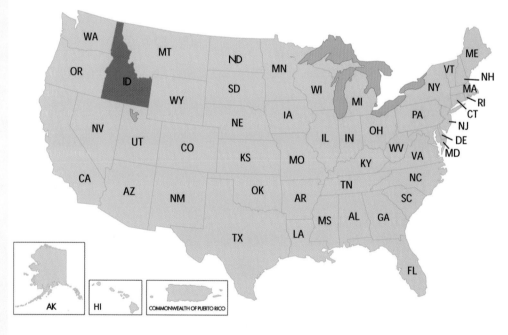

Idaho is located in the northwestern United States. It is bordered by six states and one Canadian province.

Introduction

Idaho is located in the Pacific Northwest of the United States. It is bordered by six U.S. states and one Canadian province: Washington and Oregon to the west, Nevada and Utah to the south, Montana and Wyoming to the east, and British Columbia, Canada, to the north. Idaho is the fourteenth-largest state in the United States and comprises approximately 83,642 square miles (134,609 square kilometers). It was admitted to the Union on July 3, 1890, making it the forty-third state in the country.

A state with a history of being progressive, Idaho has always been a supporter of human rights. It was one of the first states to grant women the right to vote in the late eighteenth century, and in 1914, Idaho became the first state to elect a Jewish governor, Moses Alexander.

Idaho is one of the fastest-growing states in the country. Long famous for its production of potatoes and other agricultural products, Idaho has become known in recent years for its science and technology sector. Idaho is nicknamed the Gem State due to the many different kinds of gems that can be found there.

Chapter 1

THE GEOGRAPHY OF IDAHO

Idaho features a wide variety of terrain, including snow-capped mountains, serene lakes, fertile plains, and deep canyons. The state is well known for its abundant natural resources and scenic areas, and it has some of the largest unspoiled natural regions in the country.

Larger than all of New England put together, Idaho is a mostly mountainous state regarded by locals and tourists alike as a highly outdoor-oriented community. In fact, the world's first chairlift is located in Sun Valley, a popular ski resort in central Idaho. Snow sports are so central to Idaho's identity that nearly every urban area has a ski resort nearby. Whitewater rafting and kayaking are also popular pastimes, with the town of Rigging serving as the state's informal whitewater capital.

Some believe the name "Idaho" came from a Native American word meaning "gem of the mountains." The state is home to a number of mountain ranges, including the Sawtooth Range of the Rocky Mountains and the Lost River Range. The Lost River Range boasts the highest point in the state, Borah Peak, at 12,662 feet (3,859 meters). Idaho also features Hells Canyon, the deepest canyon in North America. Carved out by the waters of the Snake River, Hell's Canyon is 7,993 feet (2,436 m) deep. It is nearly 1 mile (1.6 km) deep

Carved by the Snake River, Hells Canyon is the deepest river gorge in North America. It is a popular destination for tourists visiting Idaho.

at its western rim and sinks 8,000 feet (2,438 m) below the peaks of the Seven Devils Mountain range to the east.

Idaho is also home to many larger bodies of water. Beginning with its headwaters in Yellowstone National Park, the Snake River passes through Idaho and three other states along its 1,040-mile (1,670 kilometers) length. The 425-mile (684 km) Salmon River has rapid waters, which proved to be too rough for early explorers Meriwether Lewis and William Clark to navigate when they reached the river in 1805.

Many lakes can be found in Idaho. Bear Lake is the second-largest freshwater lake in the country and is often called the Caribbean of the Rockies due to its unique turquoise-blue color. Lake Coeur d'Alene

Hells Canyon

Hells Canyon was formed more than three hundred million years ago when a number of volcanoes emerged from the waters of the Pacific Ocean. Over millions of years, the volcanoes subsided, and the basins between them filled up with sedimentary rock.

The earliest known human inhabitants of Hells Canyon were the Nez Perce Indians. The Nez Perce found the canyon hospitable due to its mild winters and its ample plant and animal life. Later, other tribes made the canyon their home, including the Shoshone-Bannock, the Northern Paiute, and the Cayuse Indians. Fortunately, the tribes left behind many pictures and petroglyphs on the walls of the canyon so that we are able to maintain a record of their lives.

In 1806, three members of the Lewis and Clark expedition entered Hells Canyon on the Snake River. Harsh conditions soon forced them out. Five years later, the pioneer Wilson Price Hunt explored the canyon while seeking a shortcut to the Columbia River. However, hunger and cold caused the expedition to turn back.

Today, Hells Canyon serves as one of the state's main attractions for tourists and thrill-seekers. The Snake River is famous for whitewater rafting. The canyon also offers visitors opportunities for swimming, hunting, fishing, boat rides, kayaking, paragliding, and more. Established in 1965, the Hells Canyon Preservation Council works toward protecting and preserving the canyon. In 2007, the council prevented the logging of 651 acres (263 hectares) of trees near the Eagle Cap Wilderness area.

In late 2009, the Wallowa-Whitman National Forest, part of which overlaps Hells Canyon, received federal stimulus money for maintenance and repair. Beginning in 2011, the ambitious project will allow for brush to be trimmed and logs to be cleared on over 1,300 miles (2,092 km) of trail. Hikers, horseback riders, and other outdoor enthusiasts will enjoy access to new regions of Hells Canyon.

is a popular tourist spot owing to its great beaches and scenic views. Another landmark native to the state is Shoshone Falls, the waterfall located on the Snake River. Shoshone Falls is sometimes called the Niagara of the West because, at 212 ft (65 m) high, it is actually slightly higher than Niagara Falls.

Climate

Idaho's northern and western regions feel the influence of the Pacific Ocean, even though it lies about 350 miles (560 km) to the west. This influence keeps winter temperatures fairly mild and results in high cloud cover, humidity, and precipitation in the winter. Though temperatures can occasionally reach freezing (32 degrees Fahrenheit, or 0 degrees Celsius), it is rare for them to go much lower. Southwestern Idaho feels less of an effect from the ocean, meaning drier winters and wetter summers.

During the summer, much of Idaho can be very warm and dry, with low humidity levels. Temperatures rarely reach 100°F (38°C) though, and summer nights in Idaho are often cool.

Plant and Animal Life of Idaho

Idaho's unspoiled forest areas are home to a wide variety of woodland creatures. The state animal is the Appaloosa horse, a breed developed by the Nez Perce tribe. After the Nez Perce War of 1877, the breed was on the decline and in danger of becoming extinct. However, a small number of dedicated breeders worked together to keep the Appaloosa alive. Today, it is one of the most popular breeds of horses in America. Many elk, bobcats, coyotes, moose, black bears, and grizzly bears make their home in Idaho as well. Numerous

Originally bred by the Nez Perce tribe, the Appaloosa horse faced extinction after the Nez Perce War of 1877.

species of bats, rabbits, and hares can be found in the state.

Originally native to the Rocky Mountains, the gray wolf disappeared from the area in 1926 due to overhunting. The wolf was reintroduced to the area in 1995 and flourished to the point that it was removed from the federal protection list, which catalogs endangered species. However, many environmental groups worried this would lead to overhunting once again and fought to have the gray wolf returned to the list.

Idaho's well-populated lakes and rivers have long made the state an ideal spot for fishing. There are more than ten blue-ribbon wild trout streams in the state, including Henry's Fork in Island Park, Silver Creek, and the St. Joseph River. In contrast with many states, most fishing waters in Idaho are open for free to the general public.

Idaho's fertile plains host many kinds of plants and vegetation, including pincushions, salt brush, wheatgrass, dandelions, juniper, and ricegrass. The Idaho Native Plant Society was established to promote interest in the native fauna of the state and to protect rare and endangered plants. Each year, the organization sponsors the Idaho Rare Plant Conference, which brings together botanists from all over the state.

Boise is the largest city in Idaho. It has been the state capital since 1866, only two years after it was incorporated as a city.

Major Cities

Idaho has a population of about 1,524,000 people. The state is divided into 44 counties, which are further divided into 110 cities and towns. The largest city is Boise, located on the Boise River in the southwestern part of the state. Boise proper has a population of about two hundred thousand people. The Boise metropolitan area has a population of about 588,000 people. The second-largest city is Nampa, with a population of about seventy-nine thousand people. Nampa is one of the fastest-growing cities in the state. The city's name comes from a Native American word thought to mean either "footprint" or "moccasin." Another rapidly growing city, Meridian, has a population of about sixty-five thousand people and is the third-largest city in the state. Meridian experienced an 81.5 percent increase in its population from 2000 to 2009.

Natural Resources

Idaho is known as the Gem State for a good reason: Nearly every known kind of gem has been found in Idaho, including its state gem, the rare star garnet. The star garnet can only be found in Idaho and the Himalayan Mountains of India.

The discovery of gold first brought permanent settlers to Idaho Territory in 1863. After the settlers arrived, it didn't take long for the gold deposits to disappear. By the end of the century, however, silver, lead, and zinc deposits were discovered near the city of Coeur d'Alene, and today the area is one of the world's richest in minerals. In addition, the state is rich in silver and lumber resources.

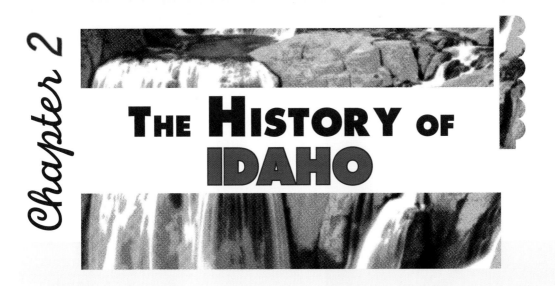

THE HISTORY OF IDAHO

Historians believe humans may have inhabited Idaho as early as 14,500 years ago. In 1959, an excavation of Wilson Butte Cave near Twin Falls, Idaho, turned up evidence of ancient human inhabitants, including arrowheads that rank among the oldest artifacts found in North America. This excavation was led by archaeologist Ruth Gruhn, and it is believed that this was the first time the artifacts had been disturbed in thousands of years.

Early Residents and Explorers

Before the arrival of European explorers, Idaho was dominated by two Native American tribes: the Nez Perce in the north and the Shoshone in the south. Like many western Native American tribes, the Nez Perce were migratory. This means they traveled with the seasons, moving to different areas depending on where the most abundant food could be found. The tribe also bred Appaloosa horses, which are now the state animal of Idaho.

At one time, the Shoshone tribe's area extended as far east as Wyoming, Montana, and Colorado. However, conflicts with the Blackfoot, Crow, Lakota, Cheyenne, and Arapaho tribes forced the Shoshone westward into Idaho, Nevada, and Utah around 1750.

Chief Joseph was the leader of the Wal-lam-wat-kain (or Wallowa) band of Nez Perce. He presided over the tribe during General Oliver O. Howard's attempt to forcibly relocate them in 1877.

The Idaho groups of Shoshone were known as Tukuaduka, meaning "sheep eaters."

In 1792, Captain George Vancouver of the British Royal Navy explored the Puget Sound in the Pacific Northwest. Captain Vancouver claimed parts of British Columbia, Oregon, Washington, and Idaho for Great Britain. This area would come to be known as Oregon Country.

In 1803, President Thomas Jefferson bought 828,000 square miles (2 million sq km) of western territory from France. This land deal, which greatly expanded the size of the United States, was known as the Louisiana Purchase. Neither the United States nor France knew exactly what this territory held. President Jefferson commissioned an expedition that would explore the newly purchased land. Jefferson selected Captain Meriwether Lewis to lead the expedition, which he hoped would shed new light on the Pacific Northwest's geography, Native American inhabitants, plant life, and wildlife. Captain Lewis chose William Clark as his partner, and their journey became known as the Lewis and Clark expedition. The expedition ended up traveling all the way to the Pacific Ocean. A young Shoshone woman from Idaho named Sacajawea served as Lewis and Clark's guide and interpreter. The expedition was indebted to her, not only for her comprehensive knowledge of the land but also for her ability to communicate with the Native Americans encountered along the way.

Native American Tension and Idaho Territory

The United States' claim to Oregon Country was based on Lewis and Clark's expedition, as well as on Captain Robert Gray's entry of the Columbia River in 1792. The Treaty of 1818 allowed both the United States and England access to parts of the territory. However, disputes still raged over who controlled what. The 1846 Oregon Treaty gave England the area that would become British Columbia, while giving the United States territory that would later become the states of Oregon, Washington, and Idaho.

On January 29, 1863, years of tension between Shoshone Indians and U.S. settlers culminated in the Bear River Massacre. The arrival of settlers from the east forced the Shoshone out of their established villages and into areas where they

Today, the site of the Bear River Massacre is marked with a stone monument to honor those who died.

Boise

Idaho's capital and most populated city, Boise, was home to Fort Boise in the early 1830s. Originally built by the Hudson's Bay Company as a trading post, Fort Boise was abandoned in 1835. A French-Canadian fur trapper named Francois Payette took over the fort, using it to provide hospitality and supplies to travelers and settlers. In 1839, Payette began construction of a second Fort Boise where the Boise River met the Snake River. However, with the demise of the fur trade in the 1850s, the fort was once again abandoned.

On July 4, 1863, the day after the Battle of Gettysburg concluded, Fort Boise was reopened by the U.S. Army to serve as a military post. The fort was constructed largely in response to the many massacres that occurred on the Oregon Trail in the years since the old fort had been abandoned. Boise was incorporated as a city in 1864 and named the capital of Idaho Territory the following year. In 1912, the National Guard took over Fort Boise and turned it over to the Public Health Service in 1919. The Public Health Service used it to house World War I veterans and tuberculosis patients.

Today, Boise is known for its business climate and the high quality of living enjoyed by its citizens. It is the headquarters for several major companies, including URS Corporation, Albertsons, and Micron Technology. In 2007, *Forbes* magazine ranked Boise third on its list of "Best Places for Business and Careers." Boise is also known as a regional hub for music and theater. Every spring, the city hosts the Gene Harris Jazz Festival. Meanwhile, thousands of people attend the annual Idaho Shakespeare Festival, which presents five plays every summer.

In November 2007, Boise city officials launched Blueprint Boise, a comprehensive system to design a new city plan for Boise. The goal is to eventually update and modernize buildings and public systems in the city. Citizens can go to Boise's official Web site to see developments posted as they happen, and post their feedback to be read by city planners.

had a hard time producing enough food. The hunting and foraging of the recently arrived pioneers further depleted Shoshone food sources. Pushed to the brink of starvation, tribes began raiding the camps of settlers for food. In retaliation, the U.S. Army attacked the Shoshone at the confluence of Bear River and Beaver Creek. Between two hundred to four hundred Native Americans were killed in the attack.

In 1863, areas of present-day Idaho, Montana, and Wyoming were organized into the Idaho Territory. For the first two years of its existence, the capital of the Idaho territory was Lewiston. In 1865, it became Boise, which remains the capital of Idaho to this day.

U.S. Statehood and World Wars

Idaho became the forty-third state to be admitted to the Union on July 3, 1890. At this time, the state's population was about 88,500, but by 1900, just ten years later, it had nearly doubled.

In 1914, Idaho made history by becoming the first state to elect a Jewish governor. Prior to getting elected as governor, Moses Alexander was the mayor of Boise, a position he held beginning in 1897. Alexander was able to accomplish a significant amount in his single term and chose not to run for re-election. He is credited for organizing the city's volunteer fire department, passing several antigambling ordinances, and making other significant improvements to the city. In 1914, Alexander entered the race for governor on a platform that strongly supported prohibition, a law that made the manufacture and sale of alcohol illegal. He won the election and would be reelected in 1916. During his tenure as governor, Alexander pledged state militia troops to help fight in World War I.

On June 30, 1917, the USS *Idaho*, a U.S. Navy battleship named after the state, was launched. Sponsored by Henrietta Amelia Simons,

The USS *Idaho* was a battleship launched in 1917. Seen here in 1940, the USS *Idaho* was awarded seven battle stars for its service in World War II.

granddaughter of Moses Alexander, the ship would patrol the Pacific Ocean during World War II. Perhaps most famously, it carried Allied troops into Tokyo Bay on August 27, 1945. The USS *Idaho* would go on to receive seven battle stars for its service in the war and earn the nickname the "Big Spud."

Contemporary Idaho

In the 1950s, Idaho's chief agricultural export, the potato, became one of the first agricultural products to be advertised on radio and television. As a result, Idaho potatoes became the most popular variety of potato in the United States. They also grew to be a key component of Idaho's economy.

The success of the potato in Idaho was only eclipsed by the technology boom of the 1970s, which Idaho was at the center of. Idaho has experienced a rapid growth of its business and industry and is one of the fastest-growing states in America. Since 1990, the state's population has increased by about 38 percent, or about 386,000 people. As of 2005, Idaho is the sixth fastest-growing state in the country, following Arizona, Nevada, Florida, Georgia, and Utah.

Chapter 3

THE GOVERNMENT OF IDAHO

Like the U.S. Constitution, the constitution of Idaho calls for the state government to be divided into three branches: executive, legislative, and judicial. Idaho still operates under its original 1889 state constitution, which was modeled after the U.S. Constitution. The state's laws are recorded in the Idaho Code, a long document collected in several volumes. Both the state constitution and code can be amended at any time by a vote of the legislature, with the approval of the governor.

The Executive Branch

The executive branch of Idaho's government includes the governor, the lieutenant governor, and the secretary of state. The governor of Idaho is the chief executive of the state. The governor and lieutenant governor are elected to four-year terms. There is no limit on the number of terms a governor may serve, and a governor can serve for as long as the public keeps voting for him or her.

The position of lieutenant governor is voted on separately from the office of governor. The lieutenant governor is first in the line of succession to the governor, meaning that if the governor is out of the state, or in any way unable to discharge his or her duties, the lieutenant governor acts as governor. The lieutenant governor also presides over the Idaho State Senate.

The secretary of state is an elected official responsible for the administration of state elections, as well as the regulation of lobbying and campaign finance. The secretary of state is responsible for making sure all elections in Idaho are run fairly and proceed as smoothly as possible.

The Legislative Branch

The Idaho State Capitol is located in downtown Boise. The capitol building was completed in 1913 using sandstone from the nearby Table Rock Quarry.

Like the United States, Idaho has a bicameral legislature, meaning the legislature is divided into two houses: the Idaho Senate and the Idaho House of Representatives. The Senate is comprised of thirty-five senators, elected from thirty-five districts. The House consists of seventy representatives, elected from the same thirty-five districts as the Senate (two are elected in each district). Senators and representatives serve two-year terms, and elections are held every even-numbered year. There are no term limits for legislators. Idaho's legislature is part-time. Because of this, Idaho's legislators are referred to as "citizen legislators," meaning that their position as a legislator is not their main occupation.

Human Rights in Idaho

Throughout American history, Idaho has always supported progressive movements and shown a strong concern for human rights. In the summer of 1848, activists, including Elizabeth Cady Stanton, Lucretia Mott, and Susan B. Anthony, began a seventy-year campaign to secure women's suffrage, or the right to vote. In the late nineteenth century, Idaho became one of just four states in the country to support women's suffrage, along with Colorado, Utah, and Wyoming. In the early twentieth century, as the battle for women's rights raged on, the National American Woman Suffrage Association adopted Idaho native Sacajawea as a symbol of their cause, claiming that the Shoshone woman represented the kind of strength and independence they were fighting for.

Today, Idaho retains a strong commitment to human rights. In 1995, a traveling exhibit called "Anne Frank and the World" came to Idaho. Anne Frank was a young Jewish girl who, along with the rest of her family, hid from the Nazis for years in an attic in Amsterdam during World War II. Her story was preserved in a diary kept during this time in hiding. The Anne Frank exhibit was on display in Idaho for one month. An enormous success, the exhibit attracted more than forty-six thousand visitors. Inspired by Idahoan's interest in human rights, the Idaho Human Rights Education Center in Boise raised $1.8 million to build its own Anne Frank memorial. In 2001, the Anne Frank Human Rights Memorial was erected in Boise's cultural district.

In 2006, the Idaho state legislature passed a title calling for a commission on human rights in the state. The following year, the governor established the Idaho Human Rights Commission, an independent agency set up to help the state legislature protect citizens from illegal discrimination. The commission seeks to secure freedom for all individuals in the state, investigate complaints of discriminatory practices in employment settings, and enact policies embodied in federal civil rights laws.

At one time, legislators were chosen from each county, but this is no longer the case. Today, districts have been created so that the number of legislators is proportional to the number of people they represent. Many districts encompass several counties, while some districts are located within a single county. The state's largest, most populous county, Ada County, contains eight districts.

The Idaho Legislature meets annually at the Idaho State Capitol in downtown Boise. Sessions last from January to mid-March, but are often extended well into May. The governor may also call for a special session at any time.

The Judicial Branch

The judicial branch of the state government is made up of a series of courts. The most powerful court in the state is the Idaho Supreme Court, which is comprised of a chief justice and four associate justices. The supreme court only hears the most important cases in the state. In addition, decisions made by supreme court judges are binding over all other courts in the state. The only other court that can reverse or modify decisions made by this court is the U.S. Supreme Court. Judges are elected in nonpartisan, statewide staggered elections and serve six-year terms.

After the Idaho Supreme Court, the next most powerful court in Idaho is the court of appeals. This court is an appellate court, meaning it is empowered to hear an appeal from a trial court or other lower court. The court of appeals hears cases assigned to it by the Idaho Supreme Court, with the exception of capital murder cases and cases involving workers' compensation laws, which can only be heard by the supreme court. The court of appeals includes four

The Idaho Supreme Court is the most powerful court in the state. The supreme court hears appeals of the final decisions of district courts.

judges: one chief judge and three associate judges. Each case is heard by a panel consisting of three of these judges. Finally, seven district courts make up the lower courts of the state. Each district court presides over several counties, and each is comprised of an administrative district judge and a trial court administrator.

THE ECONOMY OF IDAHO

Idaho's top five agricultural products are cattle, dairy products, hay, potatoes, and wheat. Beef cattle are the state's most valuable farm product, and milk is its most valuable livestock product. Though it has been a leading producer in agriculture for many years, Idaho has recently become known for its science and technology industry. Many top computer companies have plants or headquarters in Boise. As of the 2004 Census, Idaho's gross state product was $43.6 billion, and its per capita income was $26,881.

Agriculture

Idaho is famous for its potatoes. In fact, it produces nearly a third of all the potatoes consumed in the United States. In 1937, the Idaho Potato Commission was established to promote and market the state's top agricultural export. One of the committee's greatest achievements was its use of radio and television advertising. In 1959, the committee developed a "Grown in Idaho" seal to be placed on every Idaho potato. Since that time, Idaho potatoes have been the best-selling potatoes in the United States. Each year, the potato industry harvests 13 billion pounds (5.9 billion kilograms) of potatoes and contributes approximately $2.7 billion to the state economy. The

Here, farmers harvest potatoes in Idaho. For many years, agriculture was Idaho's chief industry, with the state's famous potatoes leading the way in exports.

industry employs thirty-nine thousand Idaho residents, almost 3 percent of the state's total population. The state is so proud of its top agricultural product that Idaho license plates feature the phrase "Famous Potatoes."

Idaho is also home to the world's largest factory for barrel cheese, the raw product that is made into processed cheese. In the United States, processed cheese is generally called American cheese and used in everything from cheeseburgers to grilled cheese sandwiches. Located in Gooding, the factory has a capacity of 132,277 tons (120,000 metric tons) per year and belongs to the Glanbia, a leading international cheese producer headquartered in Kilkenny, Ireland.

Taxes

Idaho has eight income tax brackets. The more money people make, the higher their tax bracket and the more taxes they have to pay. Idahoans may apply for tax credits, which allow them to receive tax compensation for taxes paid to other states. Idaho taxpayers can also receive tax credits for donations made to Idaho educational institutions, as well as for donations made to certain nonprofit youth and rehabilitation organizations. Idaho's state sales tax is 6 percent.

Idaho has a state gambling lottery, the proceeds of which go to Idaho public schools and higher education institutions. From 1990 to 2006, the lottery contributed $333.5 million to educational facilities in the state.

Science and Technology

The largest industry in Idaho is the state's science and technology sector, which accounts for over 25 percent of the state's total revenue and 70 percent of the state's total exports. Boise leads the way in this technological revolution, and the city has emerged as the epicenter of science and technology in the state. Boise is one of the United States' top producers of semiconductors, the chips and circuits present in many electrical and electronic devices.

Boise is also home to several top science and technology companies. Based in Boise, Micron Technology is among the world's top producers

Here, Mark Duncan, the president of research and development and the chief operating officer of Boise-based Micron Technology, addresses a crowd.

27

Idaho's Changing Industry

Idaho's first potato farmer was a Presbyterian missionary named Henry Harmon Spalding. Spalding had set up a mission in the town of Lapwai in 1837 and was attempting to demonstrate to the Nez Perce tribe that they could produce their own food without hunting or gathering. The Nez Perce had traditionally relied heavily on buffalo as a food source. However, hunting and other human activity had depleted the area's buffalo population to the point that the Nez Perce would need to cultivate a new food source. Spalding and the Nez Perce began this process by planting peas and potatoes. Though the first crop they planted was a failure, the next year saw more favorable weather, and visitors to the mission noted the abundant crop.

For many years, agriculture was Idaho's primary industry. Today, science and technology brings in the most annual revenue for Idaho. The Hewlett-Packard Company was founded in California in 1939 and opened a plant in Boise in the 1970s. The plant started out producing microchips and eventually began manufacturing LaserJet printers as well. As the digital age exploded, so did the production of technology resources in Idaho. Today, Idaho is now one of the leading producers of semiconductors in the world.

One of the new leading industrial producers in Idaho is Micron Technology. Micron is a multinational company best known for producing many forms of semiconductor devices, including DRAM components and flash memory. The company was founded in Boise in 1978 by Ward Parkinson, Joe Parkinson, Dennis Wilson, and Doug Pitman. One of its original benefactors was Idaho billionaire J. R. Simplot, who made his fortune in the potato business.

Micron has always focused on being a low-cost producer, which has allowed it to survive numerous collapses in the DRAM market that forced many of its competitors to leave the industries. Today, in addition to being a leading producer of semiconductors, Micron's consistent technological developments have made it one of the most prolific patent registrants in the United States.

of semiconductors and is the only U.S. producer of dynamic random access memory (DRAM) chips. Hewlett-Packard also owns a plant in Boise, which largely produces LaserJet printers. Sun Microsystems, which is a multinational vendor of computers, software, and technology services, brings in $4,000,000 in salaries annually to its employees in Boise and Pocatello, and it contributes $300,000,000 to state revenue every year.

Nearly half of the United States' silver comes from Idaho. This silver mine is located in Idaho's Silver Valley.

Boise isn't the only place the technology industry calls home in Idaho. The Dell computer company operates a call center in Twin Falls, and ON Semiconductor, a widely recognized innovator in state-of-the-art semiconductor products, is headquartered in Pocatello.

Other Industry

Other important industries in Idaho's economy include food processing, lumber, machinery, paper products, and mining. The mineral-rich areas of Coeur d'Alene help Idaho produce the most newly mined silver in the nation. Idaho produces almost 45 percent of the United States' silver and 15 percent of the country's phosphate. Although Idaho produces very little gold, there is still more gold found in Idaho than in any other state in the country.

Chapter 5

PEOPLE FROM IDAHO:
PAST AND PRESENT

Idaho has produced some of the most innovative and important individuals in U.S. history. From business to the arts to athletics, many famous people were born in Idaho or made the state their home. Idahoans have given the world the television, Mount Rushmore, and important American literature. The following are some of the notable people from the state.

Joseph Albertson (1906–1993) The founder of a chain of grocery stores and a notable philanthropist, Joseph Albertson was born in Oklahoma Territory. When he was three years old, his family moved to Boise, Idaho. He opened the first of his Albertson's grocery stores in Boise in 1939. During World War II, Albertson's stores began promoting war bonds and sponsoring scrap metal drives to raise money for U.S. troops. In the 1950s and 1960s, Albertson began expanding his grocery store chain. Shoppers throughout the western United States became familiar with Joseph Albertson's service and generosity.

Gutzon Borglum (1867–1941) Born in St. Charles, Idaho, Gutzon Borglum was an artist and sculptor best known for creating Mount Rushmore. Commissioned in 1923 by a South Dakota state historian, Borglum's first attempt at creating one of the faces lasted two years and ended in failure: He blew up his work with dynamite so that he could start again from scratch. When not overseeing the site personally, Borglum went on world tours to raise funds in order to complete the project. Today, Mount Rushmore is one of the United States' most recognizable landmarks.

Idaho native Gutzon Borglum gained recognition for his large statues and carvings in mountains. He is best remembered for designing Mount Rushmore.

Edgar Rice Burroughs (1875–1950) The creator of Tarzan, Edgar Rice Burroughs was born in Chicago, Illinois, but moved to Idaho during the Chicago flu epidemic of 1891. After being discharged from the army in 1897, Burroughs had difficulty finding a job, and during his downtime became interested in pulp fiction magazines. Inspired by the stories he found there, he began a career in writing. In 1912, Burroughs published his first Tarzan novel.

Philo Farnsworth (1906–1971) Philo Farnsworth, who would one day be considered the Father of Television, moved with his family to Rigby, Idaho, when he was just a child. At Rigby High School, Farnsworth excelled in chemistry and physics, often drawing sketches and prototypes of the

A native of Rigby, Idaho, Philo Farnsworth began researching and developing technologies in high school that would lead to the development of the television.

electron tubes that he would later use to invent the fully electronic television set. In the 1920s, he moved to Los Angeles, where he completed his invention and sold it to the RCA Victor company for $1,000,000 in 1939 (approximately $15,000,000 in today's money).

Gene Harris (1933–2000) Jazz pianist Gene Harris had already enjoyed a successful career when he retired to Boise in the late 1970s. His music career was resurrected in the 1980s, when friend and fellow jazz musician Ray Brown convinced him to go back on tour in the 1980s. He continued to tour and record albums for Concord Records up until his death in 2000. In 1996, the Gene Harris Jazz Festival was launched, and it continues to occur annually in Boise.

Harmon Killebrew (1936–) Born in Payette, Idaho, Harmon Killebrew made his Major League Baseball debut with the Washington Senators in 1954 when he was just seventeen years old. (The Senators became the Minnesota Twins in 1961.) He played with the team for most of his career, during which time he was selected for eleven All-Star teams. Killebrew was named the American League's Most Valuable Player in 1969. In 1974, his number 3 jersey became the first to be retired by the Twins franchise, and in 1984 he was inducted into the Baseball Hall of Fame.

Jake Plummer (1974–) Born in Boise, Jake Plummer began his football career as a quarterback at Arizona State. During his time at Arizona State, Plumber was named a consensus All-American and was the Pac-10 Player of the Year in

Native Americans in Idaho

Native Americans were the first inhabitants of the area that would become Idaho. When European settlers began traveling to the area in the eighteenth century, they traded goods with the Native Americans living there. Europeans also brought the first Appaloosa horses to the state, which the Nez Perce would eventually breed and train.

Unfortunately, Europeans also brought diseases like smallpox with them. Native Americans had never encountered these diseases before and therefore had no natural immunity to them. The diseases decimated many tribes, greatly reducing the Native American population. Tension between Native Americans and European settlers resulted in several wars in the late 1800s. The most notable of these battles was the Bear River Massacre, where an estimated two hundred to four hundred Shoshone Indians were killed.

After the Civil War, Native Americans living in Idaho were forced to move to reservations in Oklahoma. However, Chief Joseph of the Nez Perce tribe successfully negotiated their relocation to the Lapwai Reservation in Idaho and the Colville Reservation in Washington.

Today, many Indian tribes have organized their own departments of education, finance, and agriculture. Idaho's Native Americans remain valuable contributors to the state's culture and economy. The tribal affairs of the Nez Perce are governed by the Nez Perce Tribal Executive Committee, which was organized to represent the tribe in negotiations, administer tribal funds, and protect the health and welfare of tribal members.

The Shoshone tribes employ nearly one thousand native and non-native people in various trades, with a combined payroll of more than $30,000,000. The tribal government is increasingly focused on building the tribes' economy and ensuring the protection and enhancement of the reservation land base for generations to come.

1996. He entered the National Football League draft in 1997 and was selected in the second round by the Arizona Cardinals. Plumber played professionally for ten years with both the Cardinals and the Denver Broncos, and was twice selected as an alternate in the Pro Bowl.

Ezra Pound (1885–1972)
Born in Hailey, five years before Idaho became a state, Ezra Pound was a poet, critic, and major American literary figure. In 1908, he moved to Europe and encouraged an exchange of work and ideas among some of the most important poets and writers of

Boise-born Jake Plummer enjoyed a memorable career playing football in college before being drafted to play in the NFL. While in college, he was named a consensus All-American.

the century. For the last fifty years of his life, Pound worked on a long, book-length poem called *The Cantos*.

Marilynne Robinson (1943–) Born in Sandpoint, Idaho, author Marilynne Robinson's first book, *Housekeeping*, won the PEN/Hemingway Award for Best First Novel in 1980. In 2004, she released her second novel, *Gilead*, which won the National Book Critics Circle Award, as well as the Pulitzer Prize for fiction. She teaches writing at numerous

Sacajawea was Lewis and Clark's guide during their expedition. Sacajawea also served as a translator, allowing Lewis and Clark to communicate with the Native Americans they met.

institutions, including the University of Kent, the University of Michigan, and the Iowa Writer's Workshop.

Sacajawea (1788–1812) Born near present-day Salmon, Idaho, Sacajawea was a Shoshone woman who traveled thousands of miles from North Dakota to the Pacific Ocean as a guide for the Lewis and Clark expedition. Her knowledge of the area, its wildlife, and its native people proved invaluable to the expedition. In the early twentieth century, two hundred years after her death, the National American Woman Suffrage Association adopted her as a symbol.

Lana Turner (1921–1995) Born in Wallace, Idaho, actress Lana Turner was discovered by talent scouts and signed to a contract with MGM when she was only sixteen years old. She is best known for her work in such films as *The Bad and the Beautiful*, *Imitation of Life*, *The Postman Always Rings Twice*, and *Peyton Place*, for which she was nominated for an Academy Award for Best Actress.

Timeline

1800–1840 Early Native American cultures come in contact with European settlers.

1803 The United States purchases the Louisiana Territory from France.

1805 Meriwether Lewis and William Clark enter the area of present-day Idaho.

1818 The United States and England sign a joint occupation treaty for the Oregon Territory.

1836 Henry H. Spalding establishes a mission near Lapwai, where he grows the state's first potatoes.

1863 Idaho becomes a territory on March 4. The Bear River Massacre, the West's largest single slaughter of Native Americans, occurs near Preston.

1864 Boise is named the capital of Idaho.

1890 Idaho becomes the forty-third state on July 3.

1914 Moses Alexander becomes the first elected Jewish governor in the United States.

1917 The USS *Idaho* is launched.

1920 Philo Farnsworth, a fifteen-year-old student and inventor from Rigby, develops concepts that lead to the invention of television.

1934 Idaho becomes the United States' leading silver producer.

1939 Joe Albertson opens his first supermarket in Boise.

1984 Harmon Killebrew is inducted into the Baseball Hall of Fame.

1992 Linda Copple Trout becomes the first woman appointed to the Idaho Supreme Court.

2001 The Anne Frank Human Rights Memorial is built in Boise.

2003 The longest legislative session in state history occurs, lasting 118 days.

2005 The Nez Perce water agreement is ratified, securing tribal rights to a portion of Clearwater River.

2008 The gray wolf is taken off the federal protection list after reaching a population of 1,500. Worried that this would lead to it being hunted once again, environmentalists successfully lobbied to have the gray wolf returned to the list.

Idaho at a Glance

State motto:	*Esto perpetua* ("Let it be perpetual")
State capital:	Boise
State tree:	Western white pine
State flower:	Syringa
State bird:	Mountain bluebird
State song:	"Here We Have Idaho"
State fruit or vegetable:	Huckleberry
Statehood date and number:	July 3, 1890; forty-third state
State nickname:	The Gem State
Total area and U.S. rank:	83,642 sq miles (216,632 sq km); fourteenth-largest state
Approximate population at most recent census:	1,523,816
Major rivers:	Clark Fork/Pend Oreille River, Clearwater River, Salmon River, Snake River

State Flag

State Seal

Major lakes:	Bear Lake, Lake Coeur d'Alene, Redfish Lake, Sawtooth Lake
Origin of state name:	Unknown, but some speculate it derives from a Shoshone word meaning "gem of the mountains"
Highest elevation:	Mt. Borah, 12,662 feet (3,859.4 m)
Lowest elevation:	Lewiston, 738 feet (224.9 m)
Hottest temperature recorded:	118 degrees Fahrenheit (47.7 degrees Celsius) July 28, 1934
Coldest temperature recorded:	-60 degrees Fahrenheit (-51.1 degrees Celsius) January 16, 1943
Chief agricultural products:	Potatoes, barrel cheese
Major industries:	Science and technology, lumber and wood products, machinery, chemical products, paper products, electronics manufacturing

Mountain Bluebird

Syringa

GLOSSARY

battle star An award given to a ship in recognition of its service during wartime.

bicameral Two branches, chambers, or houses of a legislative body.

chairlift A series of chairs suspended from a motor-driven cable, used to convey skiers up the side of a slope.

commission To give an order or authorize the production of something.

constituency The voters or residents in a district, represented by an elective officer.

excavation The action of digging material out of something, especially at an archaeological site.

flourish To grow or develop in a healthy way.

forage To search for food or provisions.

garnet A precious stone consisting of a deep-red, glasslike material.

gubernatorial Relating to the office of state governor.

hospitable Friendly and welcoming to strangers and guests.

huckleberry A small, round, edible blue-black berry related to the blueberry.

Louisiana Purchase Approximately 828,800 square miles (2 million sq km) of territory that the United States purchased from France in 1803.

metropolitan Relating to a capital or chief city and its surrounding areas.

microchip A tiny wafer of semiconducting material used to make an integrated circuit.

migrate To move from one region or habitat to another.

moccasin A soft leather slipper or shoe.

nonpartisan Not biased toward any particular political group.

petroglyphs Prehistoric rock carvings.

preservation The action of maintaining something in its original state.

Prohibition A law that made the manufacture and sale of alcohol illegal in the United States. Prohibition was enacted in 1920 and overturned in 1933.

reservation Land set aside for occupation by Native Americans.

suffrage The right to vote in political elections.

wheatgrass A coarse grass with long, creeping roots.

whitewater Fast, shallow stretches of water in a river.

Basque Museum and Cultural Center
611 Grove Street
Boise, ID 83702
(208) 343-2671
Web site: http://www.basquemuseum.com
This museum has exhibits, artifacts, and information relating to the Basque community of Idaho.

Idaho Historic Preservation Council
P.O. Box 1495
Boise, ID 83701
(208) 424-5111
Web site: http://www.preservationidaho.org
This organization is dedicated to the protection and preservation of historic areas throughout the state.

Idaho Human Rights Education Center
777 S 8th Street
Boise, ID 83702
(208) 345-0304
Web site: http://www.idaho-humanrights.org
This nonprofit organization promotes human rights through education programming, Anne Frank Memorial tours, and collaborative advocacy.

Idaho Military History Museum
4748 S. Lindbergh Street
Boise, ID 83705
(208) 272-4841
Web site: http://inghro.state.id.us/museum
This museum was established to preserve and display artifacts of Idaho military history.

Idaho Museum of Mining and Geology
2455 Old Penitentiary Road
Boise, ID 83712

(208) 368-9876

Web site: http://www.idahomuseum.org

This museum offers exhibits and educational programs about Idaho's geological history and mining heritage.

Idaho Museum of Natural History

5th Street and Dillon Street, Building 12

Pocatello, ID 83209

(208) 282-3317

Web site: http://imnh.isu.edu

A division of Idaho State University, the Idaho Museum of Natural History acquires, preserves, and studies natural and cultural objects.

Idaho State Historical Society

2205 Old Penitentiary Road

Boise, ID 83712

(208) 334-2682

Web site: http://www.idahohistory.net

This organization seeks to preserve and promote Idaho's cultural heritage through libraries, museums, and exhibits.

Nez Perce County Historical Society and Museum

0306 Third Street

Lewiston, ID 83501

(208) 743-2535

Web site: http://www.npchistsoc.org

This organization works to preserve the history of Nez Perce County with a museum and publications.

Nez Perce National Historical Park

39063 U.S. Highway 95

Spalding, ID 83540

(208) 843-7003

Web site: http://www.nps.gov/nepe

This historical park comprises thirty-eight sites belonging to the Nez Perce tribe and commemorates Nez Perce history, stories, and culture.

State of Idaho Parks and Recreation

P.O. Box 83720

Boise, ID 83720

(208) 334-4199

Web site: http://www.parksandrecreation.idaho.gov

This organization manages all parks and recreation in Idaho and provides literature on the state's attractions and wildlife.

Web Sites

Due to the changing nature of Internet links, Rosen Publishing has developed an online list of Web sites related to the subject of this book. This site is updated regularly. Please use this link to access the list:

http://www.rosenlinks.com/uspp/idpp

Aiken, Katherine G. *Idaho's Bunker Hill: The Rise and Fall of a Great Mining Company 1885–1981*. Norman, OK: University of Oklahoma Press, 2007.

Alt, David D. *Roadside Geology of Idaho*. Missoula, MT: Mountain Press Publishing Company, 1989.

Derig, Betty B. *Roadside History of Idaho*. Missoula, MT: Mountain Press Publishing Company, 1996.

Evancho, Joe. *Fishing Idaho: An Angler's Guide*. Boise, ID: Cutthroat Press, 2004.

Fleisher, Kass. *The Bear River Massacre and the Making of History*. Albany, NY: State University of New York Press, 2004.

Heaton, John W. *The Shoshone-Bannocks: Culture and Commerce at Fort Hall, 1870–1940*. Lawrence, KS: University Press of Kansas, 2005.

Kukla, John. *A Wilderness So Immense: The Louisiana Purchase and the Purchase of the Destiny of America*. New York, NY: Anchor Press, 2004.

Lewis, Meriwether, and William Clark. *The Journals of Lewis and Clark* (Lewis & Clark Expedition). New York, NY: Mariner Books, 1997.

Macgregor, Carol Lynn. *Boise, Idaho 1882–1910: Prosperity in Isolation*. Missoula, MT: Mountain Press Publishing Company, 2006.

McConnell, W. J. *Early History of Idaho*. Aurora, CO: Bibliographical Center for Research, 2009.

Penson-Ward, Betty. *Idaho Women in History: Big and Little Biographies and Other Gender Stories*. Boise, ID: Legendary Publishing Company, 1990.

Ream, Lanny R. *The Gem & Mineral Collector's Guide to Idaho*. Baldwin Park, CA: Gem Guides Book Company, 2000.

Rember, John. *Traplines: Coming Home to Sawtooth Valley*. London, England: Vintage Books, 2004.

Robertson, R. G. *Idaho Echoes in Time*. Boise, ID: Tamarack Books, 1998.

Rowland, Della. *The Story of Sacajawea: Guide to Lewis and Clark*. New York, NY: Yearling Books, 1989.

Schwantes, Carlos Arnaldo. *In Mountain Shadows: A History of Idaho*. Lincoln, NE: University of Nebraska Press, 1991.

Tekiela, Stan. *Birds of Idaho Field Guide*. Cambridge, MN: Adventure Publications, 2003.

Walker, Deward E. *Indians of Idaho*. Moscow, ID: University of Idaho Press, 1978.

BIBLIOGRAPHY

Carter, Alden R. *The Shoshoni*. New York, NY: Watts Publishing Group, 1989.

Desert Research Institute. "Idaho Climate Summaries." Retrieved July 7, 2009 (http://www.wrcc.dri.edu/summary/climsmid.html).

Donaldson, Thomas. *Idaho of Yesterday*. Westport, CT: Greenwood Press, 1970.

Kummer, Patricia K. *Idaho*. Mankato, MN: Capstone High/Low Books, 1999.

Idaho State Historical Society. "Idaho History Time." Retrieved July 8, 2009 (http://www.idahohistory.net/dateline.html).

Jones, Landon Y. *The Essential Lewis and Clark*. New York, NY: Harper Perennial, 2002.

Office of the Governor, The State of Idaho. "Idaho History." Retrieved July 8, 2009 (http://gov.idaho.gov/fyi/history/history_index.html).

Peterson, F. Ross. *Idaho: A Bicentennial History*. New York, NY: Norton, 1976.

Pomeroy, Earl. *The Pacific Slope: A History of California, Oregon, Washington, Idaho, Utah, and Nevada*. Reno, NV: University of Nevada Press, 2003.

Press, Petra. *The Nez Perce*. Minneapolis, MN: Compass Point Books, 2002.

Shallat, Todd. *Snake: The Plain and Its People*. Boise, ID: Boise State University Press, 1994.

State of Idaho. "Government." Retrieved July 5, 2009 (http://www.accessidaho.org/government).

U.S. Census Bureau. "State and County Quick Facts: Idaho." Retrieved July 5, 2009 (http://quickfacts.census.gov/qfd/states/16000.html).

U.S. Department of Labor. "Economy at a Glance: Idaho." Retrieved July 7, 2009 (http://www.bls.gov/eag/eag.id.htm).

Vexler, Robert I. *Chronology and Documentary Handbook of the State of Idaho*. Cary, NC: Oceana Publications, 1978.

INDEX

About the Author

John Stanley has an M.F.A. from New York University, as well as a certificate from the National Critics Institute. He has been the recipient of fellowships from the Kennedy Center and the Eugene O'Neill Theater Center. Stanley is an avid traveler who has visited forty-nine out of fifty U.S. states (with Hawaii being the lone exception), including Idaho, where he went whitewater rafting on the Snake River. He lives in Brooklyn.

Photo Credits

Cover (top left), p. 31 Library of Congress Prints and Photographs Division; cover (top right) © www.istockphoto.com/Jason Lugo; cover (bottom), p. 4 © GeoAtlas; pp. 7, 26 Shutterstock.com; pp. 3, 6, 13, 20, 25, 30, 38 © www.istockphoto.com/ Mark Pruitt; p. 10 Marilyn Angel Wynn/Nativestock.com/Getty Images; p. 11 Randy Wells/Stone/Getty Images; p. 14 MPI/Getty Images; p. 15 http:// en.wikipedia.org/wiki/Bear_River_Massacre; p. 18 Bob Landry/Time & Life Pictures/Getty Images; p. 21 © www.istockphoto.com/Alice Scully; p. 24 © Shirley Throop, Boise, Idaho; p. 27 © AP Images; p. 29 krtphotoslive/Newscom.com; p. 32 Time & Life Pictures/Getty Images; p. 35 Brian Bahr/Getty Images; p. 36 Joe Sohm/ Visions of America/Photodisc/Getty Images; p. 39 (left) Courtesy of Robesus Inc.; p. 40 Wikipedia.

Designer: Les Kanturek; Photo Researcher: Amy Feinberg